These
HAPPY-ASS VIBES
belong to:

Today is
YOUR
fucking
day!

ZEN as F*CK

A JOURNAL FOR PRACTICING THE MINDFUL ART OF NOT GIVING A SH*T

Monica Sweeney

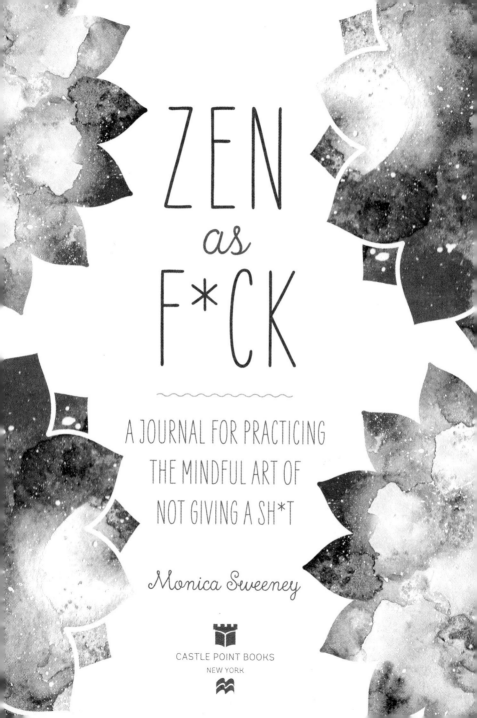

CASTLE POINT BOOKS
NEW YORK

The Castle Point Books trademark is owned by Castle Point Publications, LLC.
Castle Point books are published and distributed by St. Martin's Press.

ISBN 978-1-250-14770-7 (trade paperback)

Design by Katie Jennings Campbell

Our books may be purchased in bulk for promotional, educational,
or business use. Please contact your local bookseller or the Macmillan Corporate
and Premium Sales Department at 1-800-221-7945, extension 5442,
or by e-mail at MacmillanSpecialMarkets@macmillan.com.

First Edition: March 2018

INTRODUCTION

Welcome, sparkling person! Let me introduce you to a special form of positivity: the kind that inspires dazzling joy, cheerful catharsis, and a shit-ton of profanity. In the pages of this book, you'll find opportunities to let go of the bullshit, to pay tribute to your unique strengths, quirks, and general awesomeness, and to wave happy little flags to celebrate all of the good shit around you.

Hopscotch along this friendly path of positivity any way you like: page by page or all over the place. Be thoughtful as you consider each topic, no matter how serious or silly. Nobody likes a liar, so be honest with your answers! With a zippy fucking attitude, a smidge of serenity, and a healthy dose of vulgarity, free yourself from the bullshit and enjoy what's ahead.

Come on in, the water's delightful as fuck.

BREATHE IN STRENGTH, BREATHE OUT BULLSHIT.

WE ALL HAVE BAD DAYS.

Make a list of things that bothered you today.

_____

_____

_____

_____

_____

Then, cross that list out and
TELL IT TO FUCK OFF.

Make another list of what made today great.

_____

_____

_____

_____

_____

_____

SET GOALS *and* CRUSH THEM.

You're on top of the world:
Make a list of 5 things that make you
FUCKING FANTASTIC.

"When you walk up to opportunity's door —
don't knock on it. Kick that bitch in,
smile and introduce yourself."

—DWAYNE JOHNSON

Rise, shine, and kick ass.

ZEN AS FUCK.

WHO'S YOUR YAS QUEEN?

Think of one person who has made your world just a little bit better.
Write down the feeling they give you in a word or two.

Get your decorative pens and decorate the fuck out of this page.

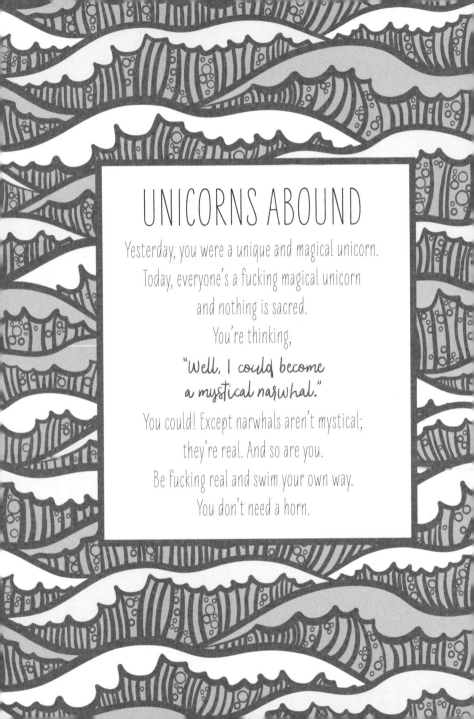

UNICORNS ABOUND

Yesterday, you were a unique and magical unicorn.
Today, everyone's a fucking magical unicorn
and nothing is sacred.
You're thinking,

*"Well, I could become
a mystical narwhal."*

You could! Except narwhals aren't mystical;
they're real. And so are you.
Be fucking real and swim your own way.
You don't need a horn.

NOW, COLOR IN THIS CUTE LITTLE GUY!

SUPERCALIFRAGILISTIC EXPIALI-DOUCHES

How often do you run into some truly atrocious people?

A lot?

While burning bridges is generally inadvisable, you don't have to keep crossing them. Think of the prickly people on your social media feed who bring you the most frustration.

FUCK 'EM!

Surround yourself with people who challenge you in healthy ways, bring you happiness, and who encourage you—not the ones who bring you negativity.

Sing a little song as you joyfully "unfriend" or "unfollow" each of these SUPERCALIFRAGILISTICEXPIALI-DOUCHES.

Um-dittle-ittl-um-dittle-I!

SHINE ON, MOTHERFUCKER

The sun gives us warmth, life, and new days.
It makes us think of new beginnings, of happy horizons,
and bright shit that sends butterflies fluttering
and precious little bunnies frolicking.
It gives some of us great fucking tans and others red-hot kisses
of scorched flesh. (Hey, it can't all be good, can it?)
Think about all the ways you can wake up, feel the sun shining,
and shine your own rays all over the place to
bring yourself and others a shit-ton of happiness.

Write one of those ways down here:

_____

_____

_____

Now, check off a bunch of boxes to make it legit!

☐ I am a ray of fucking sunshine

☐ I am a ray of fucking sunshine

☐ I am a ray of fucking sunshine

☐ I'm not always a ray of fucking sunshine, but I'll accept other people's rays on me.

SAGE IS SAID TO HAVE HEALING AND CLEANSING PROPERTIES.

Time to get new agey and pick up some dried white sage from your local farmer's market or your Internet machine. Light that shit, and let the slow-burning embers bring the sage's soothing aromas to your hopelessly jaded senses. Slowly walk around your home, passing through doorways and lingering in places that are stressful and need a little love (like the hallways you're always rushing down and the bedroom you're not having sex in). Burning sage, lighting candles and incense, and practicing aromatherapy are all ways to cleanse your home and restore the ever-elusive tranquility everyone is after. Does it work? No fucking clue, but now your house smells super lovely and you feel fucking great.

If you fuck with my

PEACE,

I'll cut a bitch.

SPREAD THOSE BEAUTIFUL
Fucking Wings

Like Icarus who flew too close to the sun,
sometimes we make decisions
that are dumb as fuck
in an attempt to get what we want.
So, start by lightening your load.
Is there something weighing on you
that's not necessary, unhealthy,
or heavy as fuck?

*"You wanna fly, you got to give
the shit up that weighs you down."*

— *SONG OF SOLOMON*, TONI MORRISON

Make a list of 3 things that are preventing you from getting where you want to be. They can be big or small.

(In Icarus' case: lofty dreams, general hubris, and a poorly designed flying apparatus.)

_____

_____

_____

Now, try to cross out at least one
of those things out of your life.
Once you've done that, try and cross out the next,
and repeat until you've finished and your load is lifted.

SPREAD YOUR STRONG AND STURDY WINGS,
AND FUCKING SOAR.

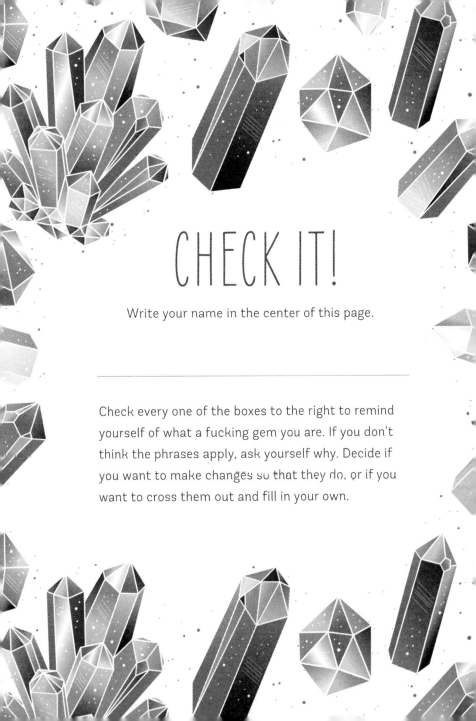

CHECK IT!

Write your name in the center of this page.

Check every one of the boxes to the right to remind yourself of what a fucking gem you are. If you don't think the phrases apply, ask yourself why. Decide if you want to make changes so that they do, or if you want to cross them out and fill in your own.

- [ ] I am fucking incredible.
- [ ] I am fucking smart.
- [ ] I am fucking powerful.
- [ ] I am fucking strong.
- [ ] I am fucking joyous.
- [ ] I am fucking lovely.
- [ ] I am fucking generous.
- [ ] I am fucking nice to people.
- [ ] I am fucking_____.
- [ ] I am fucking fair.
- [ ] I am fucking thoughtful.
- [ ] I am fucking resilient.
- [ ] I am fucking fierce.
- [ ] I am fucking great.
- [ ] I have fucking gifts to share.

- [ ] I have fucking hands to help others.
- [ ] I am fucking amazing.
- [ ] I have fucking _____.
- [ ] I am a fucking boss.
- [ ] I have fucking leadership skills.
- [ ] I am fucking exceptional.
- [ ] I am fucking wholehearted.
- [ ] I am a fucking hard worker.
- [ ] I am fucking gifted.
- [ ] I am fucking kind.
- [ ] I have fucking things to say.
- [ ] I have fucking dreams.
- [ ] I have fucking plans.
- [ ] I am fucking loving.
- [ ] I am fucking loved.

HELLO, CLARICE.

WHAT ARE THE THINGS THAT KEEP YOU UP AT NIGHT?
Your job, your family, your love life, your finances—a fictional
serial killer from the 90s? The shit that jolts you awake or
keeps you from having a second of goddamn peace may
feel like a nightmare, but it doesn't mean you can't turn it
around for the better.

For each category, list one small action that you can do
to make your hellish stressors a little bit easier.

JOB

_____

FAM

_____

LOVE

_____

MONEY

_____

DREAMS are for DICKBAGS

DON'T GET STUCK IN YOUR DREAM STATE.
While dreams are the heart and soul of any new idea,
of any new adventure, or of any bridge you haven't yet
crossed, they're also completely fucking useless if you
don't do anything with them. What are the dreams you
want to make reality? Are they achievable? Are they
batshit insane? Make a list. See what dreams you can
actually live. BE A DOER, NOT A DICKBAG!

	Achievin' is Believin'!	A li'l Batshit
	☐	☐
	☐	☐
	☐	☐
	☐	☐
	☐	☐

"You can dream a little dream or you can live a little dream. I'd rather live it, 'cause dreamers always chase but never get it."

—"NO REGRETS," AESOP ROCK

TO THOSE FUCKERS WHO TELL YOU
Everything Happens for a Reason

THERE IS NOTHING MORE INFURIATING than having something terrible happen, and some well-intentioned ass-hat pats your shoulder and says, "Don't worry, everything happens for a reason."

While this person likely meant well, this kind of response is dismissive of your feelings, unhelpful, and truly a bit fucking lazy on their part.

So, let's start with what you wanted them to say.
What would have made you feel better in that situation?
How could they have met you at your level?

WRITE IT IN THE CLOUDS, WHERE THEY CAN SOAK UP ALL YOUR FRUSTRATION.

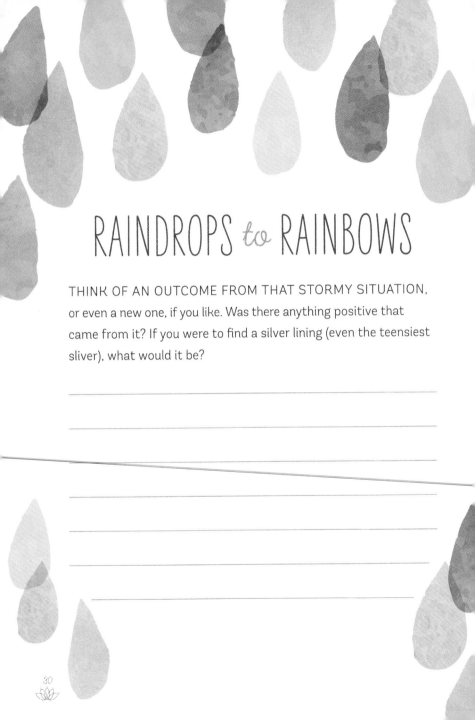

RAINDROPS to RAINBOWS

THINK OF AN OUTCOME FROM THAT STORMY SITUATION, or even a new one, if you like. Was there anything positive that came from it? If you were to find a silver lining (even the teensiest sliver), what would it be?

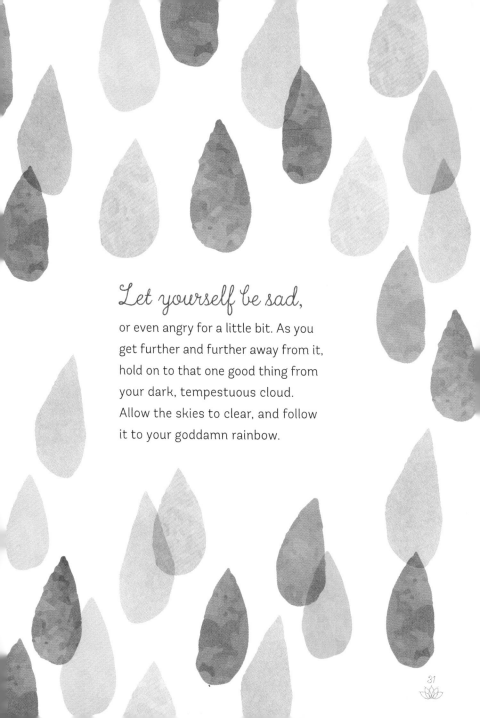

Let yourself be sad,

or even angry for a little bit. As you
get further and further away from it,
hold on to that one good thing from
your dark, tempestuous cloud.
Allow the skies to clear, and follow
it to your goddamn rainbow.

EFF-YOU HAIKU

Some people are naturally gifted at poetry.

For the rest of the population, poetry is a special form of torture designed only to remind us that we're all illiterate idiots milling about until we die.

ENTER: THE HAIKU.

Haikus are fun! They're easy! They're a great way to get some stuff off your chest. Has something or someone been bothering you lately? Get your catharsis on and write them an Eff-You Haiku. Let it out on paper, but don't actually send it to them. Because that would be rude.

TITLE

FIVE SYLLABLES

SEVEN SYLLABLES

FIVE SYLLABLES

FRANKENFEELZ

INNER DEMONS, BE DAMNED! What are qualities about yourself that sometimes make you feel like a fucking monster?

Don't be afraid of those demons.

Show a little love, and pat those monsters on the head. What do you find works best to tame them?

_____

_____

_____

_____

_____

_____

_____

Sorry, NOT SORRY

SOME THINGS REQUIRE APOLOGIES. If you've been hurtful, negligent, destructive (or you've just generally been a thoughtless dick), you should hold yourself accountable and say you're sorry. But in a world where "sorry" has become a verbal space-filler or a knee-jerk response to simply existing, saying it for everything tells the world around you that you're an inconvenience, that you're getting in the way, that you're somehow not worth someone else's time. Well, fuck that, my friend! You're worth all those things and more.

Here are some things that DO NOT require your sorrys. **Add your own!**

I am not sorry for...

- ☐ Walking through a door someone opens for me
- ☐ Accomplishing something
- ☐ Coughing
- ☐ _____
- ☐ Laughing
- ☐ Smiling
- ☐ Breathing
- ☐ _____
- ☐ Speaking up
- ☐ Speaking out
- ☐ Having ideas
- ☐ _____
- ☐ Applying myself

- ☐ _____
- ☐ Being a leader
- ☐ Frowning
- ☐ Having goals
- ☐ Having dreams
- ☐ _____
- ☐ Being opinionated
- ☐ Talking
- ☐ _____
- ☐ Passing someone
- ☐ _____

THANKS A MILLION

Who are the people you're
most thankful for?

What do you appreciate most about them?

_____

_____

_____

_____

_____

_____

_____

_____

_____

_____

_____

_____

_____

_____

_____

_____

How would you feel if someone wrote those things about you?
Pretty fucking great? Yes, so tell them.

Make them feel FUCKING GREAT.

Sweet
PICKIN'S

What is something someone said about you or to you
that made you feel like the contents of a dumpster?

What's one thing someone said about you or
to you that made you feel incredible?

_____

_____

_____

_____

_____

_____

_____

_____

_____

_____

_____

Scribble out the first one with abandon. Circle the second one,
say it out loud, and take in all its goodness.

Welcome to cherry-picking your feelings!

ENJOY THAT SWEET, SWEET FRUIT.

This Is Why We Can't

HAVE NICE THINGS

WHEN WAS THE LAST TIME YOU OVERREACTED?

_____

_____

_____

_____

On a scale of 1 to Human Tornado,
how destructive was your overreaction?

_____

Let that wind die down.

Take a deep breath, and let it out like an ocean breeze.
Maybe make yourself an umbrella drink, too.

"Tell the negative committee that meets inside your head to sit down and shut up."

— ANN BRADFORD

MEGA-POSITIVE THOUGHTS

For every negative thought you have in your head about yourself, there's a positive one scrambling behind it vying for a chance to speak. Give those positive thoughts a fucking megaphone. What are they trying to tell you?

_____

_____

_____

_____

_____

_____

_____

_____

_____

DON'T *be an* IDIOT

Not being an idiot can be hard. From sending that ill-advised text, to staying out for that one extra drink, there's always that moment that moves us from being a normal person, to being an idiot. So, take that moment to say instead, "I am not an idiot!" Write down some ways you can avoid this terrible mischaracterization in the future:

_____

_____

_____

_____

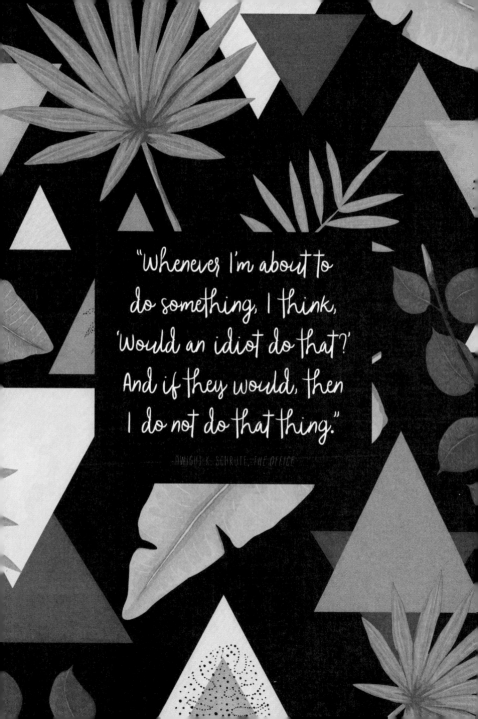

"Whenever I'm about to do something, I think, 'Would an idiot do that?' And if they would, then I do not do that thing."

DWIGHT K. SCHRUTE, THE OFFICE

GTFO

If you could pack your bags right now
and go somewhere, where would it be?

_____

Whether it's the other side of the world or the other
side of town, how could you make it happen?

_____

_____

_____

_____

_____

_____

_____

Take a Fucking
COMPLIMENT

But really.

What are some genuinely nice things* people have
said to you that you've deflected for no reason?

*Not to be confused with someone being creepy AF.

_____

_____

_____

_____

_____

_____

The next time someone gives you a compliment,
accept that shit. Use one of these handy phrases to do so:

THANKS!
WHY, THANK YOU!
GRACIAS

HOW KIND!
MERCÍ
YAS

LI'L BABY BUCKET LIST

THE NOT-QUITE-BUCKET-LIST, this is the mini version.
Make a list of things you can do in the near future that would
be super fucking fun. It doesn't have to be life-changing, but
it should be something you've been too lazy to do otherwise.
Then do those things, obviously.

1. _____

2. _____

3. _____

4. _____

5. _____

6. _____

7. _____

8. _____

9. _____

10. _____

Thank you for
saving my ass.

There is at least one person who has done this for you.

Your co-worker? Your best friend? Your sibling? Who is that person who gets your shit together for you so you don't have to?

_____

How could you have done what they did?

_____

_____

_____

_____

_____

Tell them thanks!

YOU NEVER KNOW WHEN YOU COULD GET HIT BY A BUS

SO SAY,
"I love you,"
DAMMIT!

TELL YOUR PEOPLE THAT YOU LOVE THEM. Whether it's your partner, your parents, or the nice lady who gets your coffee order right every time—let them know you care. Practice it here:

VICE CITY

Maybe you buy a lot of scratch tickets.
Maybe you enjoy a nice cocktail or seven.
Or maybe you're the person who posts endless shit
on their social media feed all the time.
If we didn't have vices, we'd be boring as fuck.

Fill in these boxes with a few of your favorite nefarious activities.

Cross out one you can live without—either for one day
or one instance. What can you replace it with
that might make your grandma* proud?

*or other kindly person who doesn't think you're an asshole

"Don't you just feel like an octopus sometimes?!"

—SOME LADY AT STARBUCKS JUGGLING BAGS, COFFEES, AND SCREAMING CHILDREN WHO HAD IT WAY HARDER THAN ME

OCTOPUS of DOOM

Being a squishy and amorphous sea creature isn't all it's cracked up to be. Sometimes we have our grimy tentacles on so much shit, we get pulled in every different direction. What are eight things that you feel like you're stuck to?

_____   _____

_____   _____

_____   _____

_____   _____

Can you pry off any of those tentacles? Which ones?

 CIRCLE THEM.

Unstick yourself, and go on and glide through that crystal-clear water like the friendly ocean-dweller you are.

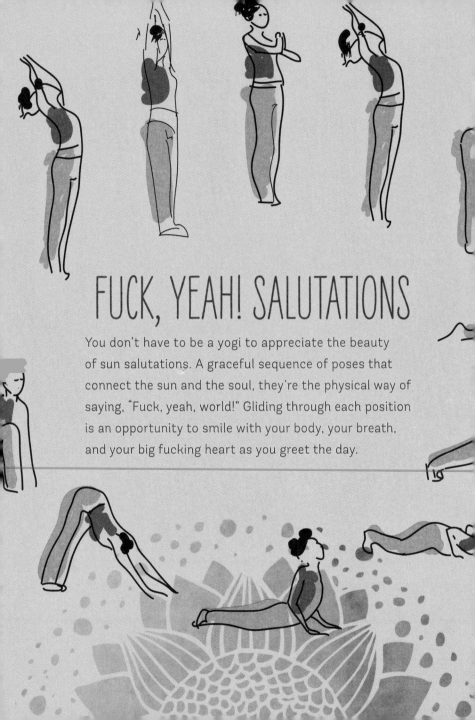

FUCK, YEAH! SALUTATIONS

You don't have to be a yogi to appreciate the beauty of sun salutations. A graceful sequence of poses that connect the sun and the soul, they're the physical way of saying, "Fuck, yeah, world!" Gliding through each position is an opportunity to smile with your body, your breath, and your big fucking heart as you greet the day.

What are three things that make you go, "Fuck, yeah!" that
can help you start your day? Try your own sun salutations,
and hold these in your thoughts with each flowing transition.

_____

_____

_____

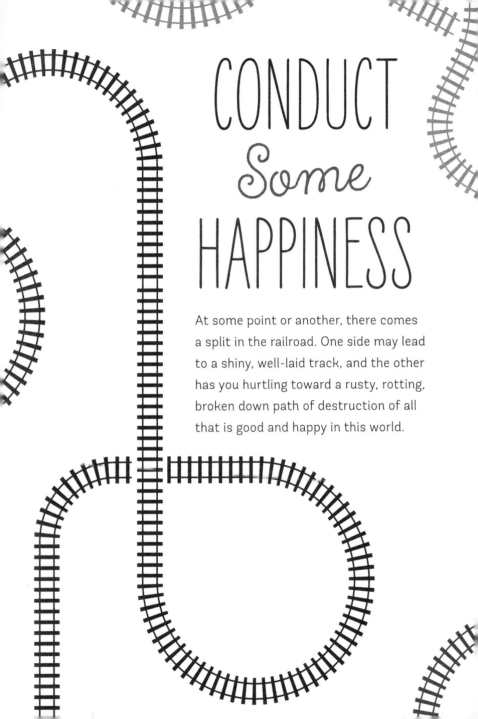

CONDUCT *Some* HAPPINESS

At some point or another, there comes a split in the railroad. One side may lead to a shiny, well-laid track, and the other has you hurtling toward a rusty, rotting, broken down path of destruction of all that is good and happy in this world.

What is something you want to see
on the smoother track?

_____

_____

_____

_____

_____

IMAGINE YOU'RE THE CONDUCTOR

(Hat included!)

What is something you can do to
steer yourself in that direction?

_____

_____

_____

_____

_____

FRAME-FUCKING-TASTIC

SET YOUR FAVORITE QUALITIES ABOUT YOURSELF in each of the purple frames, and your favorite qualities about the people you love in the gold ones. What makes you and your people fucking fantastic? Take in the variety on your gallery wall, and admire them like works of art.

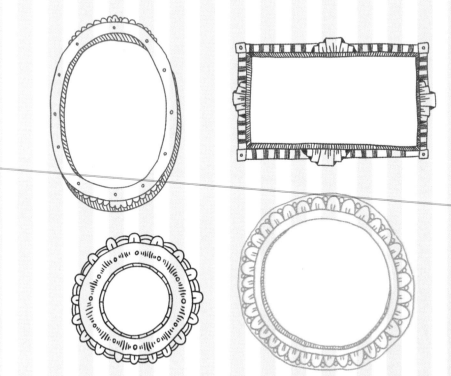

HELLO, HABITAT!

HOME IS A FEELING, a cozy blanket, a group of people you love and occasionally yell at. It can be bolted to the ground, or it can move wherever the fuck you want it to go.

What do you want your home to be built from?

_____

_____

Who makes you feel most at home?

_____

_____

_____

ONE-UPSMANSHIP
and other BULLSHIT

You fell in a puddle? I fell in a pond.
You won an award? I won two.

Whatever it is that you or those around you feel the need to one-up people about,

IT'S TIME TO CUT THAT SHIT OUT.

If you're prone to this habit, how can you avoid it in the future?

_____

_____

_____

_____

_____

When someone does this to you, take a breath before you
get pissed off and unleash all hell. They're being a dick!
But maybe they don't realize it. What are some ways you
can politely respond, or move on?

_____

_____

_____

_____

_____

May Your Cup
RUNNETH THE
FUCK OVER

Let's give a toast.
Is there someone or something
that makes you feel all fuzzy
and warm about the future?

CHEERS! ·Salud! L'chaim!

If you were to share your optimism for what comes next by clanking some dranks, what would you say?

_____

_____

_____

_____

_____

PROST! Fuck, yeah!

LET THAT SHIT GO

What are some things you're carrying that stress
you out or make you feel inadequate?

_____

_____

_____

_____

_____

_____

_____

PUT THEM IN THE BASKET OF A HAPPY FUCKING BALLOON.

Send them off into the atmosphere,

and let that shit fly far, far away.

SUFFER *or* SURF

THE OCEAN TIDE IS MUCH LIKE MOTHER NATURE HERSELF: beautiful, enigmatic, and not to be fucking ignored. You can let the waves crash on you, or you can hop up on the board and ride them out.

What waves are coming your way?

_____

_____

_____

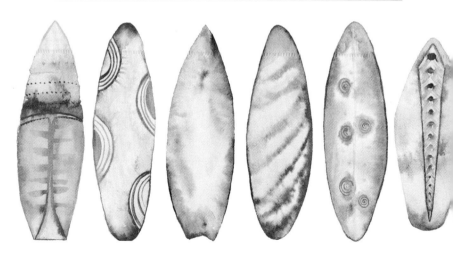

How can you take control and glide
your way back to shore?

_____

_____

_____

_____

_____

_____

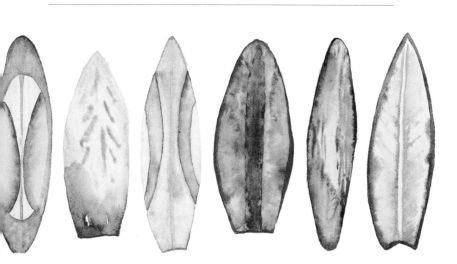

YOU GET A MILESTONE!
AND *YOU* GET A MILESTONE!

AT SOME POINT OR ANOTHER, you're going to see a stampede of people you know hit a milestone that you missed, fell short on, or that you didn't even realize you were supposed to head toward. Fuck the milestones! Maybe you'll hit them, and maybe you won't. For every milestone that someone else hit, you probably have one that they didn't. Let them happen when the time is right for you, and don't base your route on the one someone else is taking.

What are a few things you've done that made you happy? Smile at that shit!

_____

_____

_____

_____

_____

_____

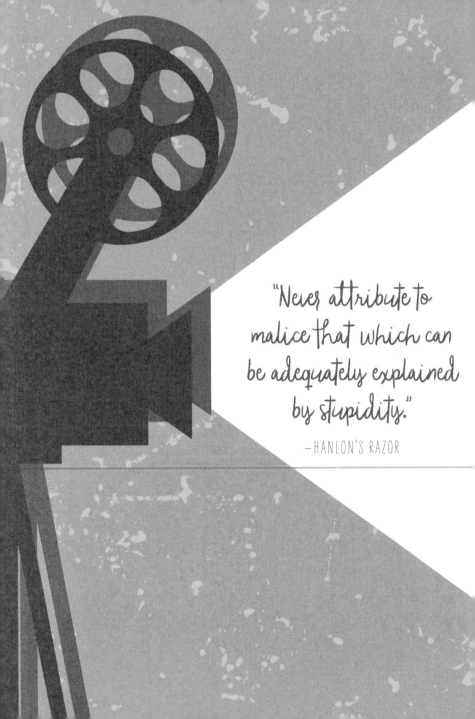

"Never attribute to malice that which can be adequately explained by stupidity."

—HANLON'S RAZOR

DUMBEREST

SOMETIMES WE ASSUME THE WORST IN PEOPLE.
Indeed, some people are the worst with a capital W, and others
are well-meaning, but just downright oblivious. Make a list of
your favorite dumb quotes from movies, books, or television.
Let this silliness offset the frustration you feel from the people
in your life who do stupid and hurtful things.

Late-Onset
COMFORT OBJECT

THERE IS NO GREATER TRUTH TO BE FOUND in the human condition than a small child having a total fucking meltdown. You look at their red little faces, bulging eyes, and hear their unholy wails rattling the earth in a supermarket aisle and you think, *That's how I feel!*

As an adult, you're generally expected to keep those moments of emotional unravelling to yourself. But it's going to be okay. What cozy comforts do you cling to in moments of stress? A comfy blanket? A fluffy pet? Your Netflix queue?

IT'S QUIET TIME

TAKE A MOMENT FOR SOME TRANQUILITY. Color in this mandala with shades that make you happy and feel at ease. Stay within the lines, because you're not a fucking animal. Enjoy this peaceful time—just you and some art.

"Try again.
Fail again.
Fail better."

—WORSTWARD HO,
SAMUEL BECKETT

FAILURE!

FAILING AT EVERYTHING sure does seem like the universe's way of telling us to fuck off. Curse those stars! What are some things that haven't quite worked out, but could use another try?

Find Your
HAPPY LITTLE TREES

WE CAN'T ALL BE ARTISTS—*swish swish swishing* our brushes to make beautiful landscapes, puffy clouds, and green mountain forests into special realms of imagination. Luckily for you, creativity means you can do just about whatever the fuck you want. Tap into your inner Bob Ross by listing off ways that you can add some imagination to your world next to these happy little leaves.

"I love to see a young girl go out and grab the world by the lapels. Life's a bitch. You've got to go out and kick ass."

–MAYA ANGELOU

SHIT-TON of INSPIRATION

WHAT ARE SOME OF THE MOST INSPIRING THINGS
you've ever heard? Take note of the quotes, motivations, or
songs that jazz you up and make you want to take the world
by fucking storm.

Pretty Soon,
WE'LL ALL BE DEAD

COME WHAT MAY—a meteor, rising sea swells, or an especially murderous banana peel—take comfort in the fact that eventually, none of the bullshit will matter. Make a list of a few things that have been really frustrating or stressful, but that you know are just temporary.

_____

_____

_____

_____

_____

_____

_____

Let those worries die.
Bury them, cremate them, or give them a nice Viking funeral!

"I am a woman with thoughts and questions and shit to say. I say if I'm beautiful. I say if I'm strong. You will not determine my story—I will."

—AMY SCHUMER

NO-NONSENSE NARRATIVE

Fuck what other people think.

Fill this page with your words about your story—
not someone else's.

_____

_____

_____

_____

_____

_____

_____

_____

_____

_____

_____

_____

_____

_____

_____

_____

_____

Ask, and You Shall Receive, MAYBE

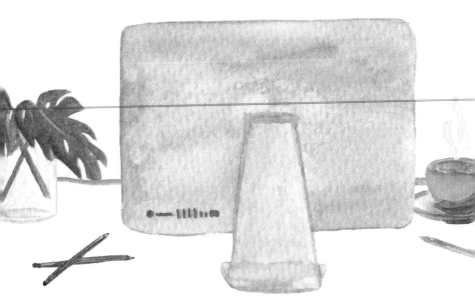

NO ONE HAS EVERYTHING THEY WANT FROM THEIR CAREER. Some people are swimming in cash, some people have a happy work culture, rewarding projects, or their very own bean bag chair, and other people have lots and lots of exposure! While you can't have everything, you definitely can't have anything if you don't fucking ask. What are some reasonable things that would make you happier or help you grow at your job? Write them down. Set a date. Use those words and ask!

QUACK QUACK, MOTHERFUCKER

PADDLE INTO 5 MINUTES OF SILENCE. Let your thoughts drift around like a cute little duck on still waters. Float your fucking heart out. After the 5 minutes are up, record some of your thoughts.

_____

_____

_____

_____

What thoughts annoyed you?

_____

_____

_____

What made you most content?

_____

_____

_____

THE PURGE

A LITTLE CATHARSIS IS NECESSARY NOW AND THEN.
What are the things that drive you fucking insane? Write them
in the boxes. Take them in for a moment, and then scribble
them out with a marker. Enjoy your abstract work of art that
is free from the things you despise most.

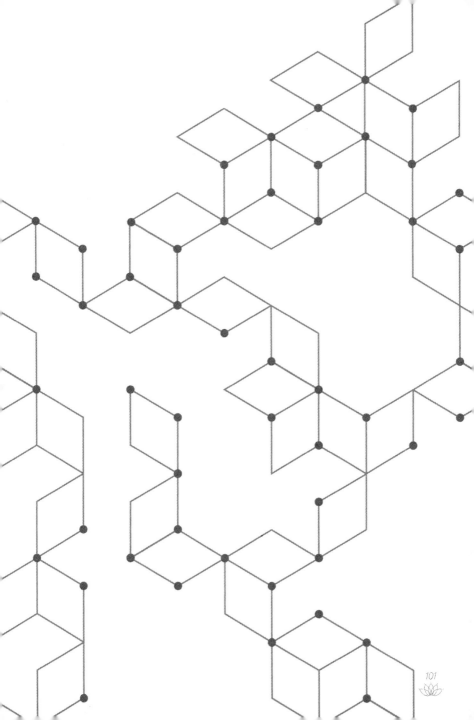

Delicious

FUCKING TREATS,

Please

WHAT IS ONE MEAL, SNACK, OR DELICIOUS FOOD stuff you've eaten that has made your goddamn day? Don't wait for someone else to serve it to you—make it yourself. Jot down the recipe here, and plan a time to Julia Child the shit out of it. Count it as happiness calories.

Ingredients

_____

_____

_____

_____

Recipe

_____

_____

_____

_____

_____

Notes

_____

_____

_____

RIGHT ON, RITUAL

CLEARING YOUR MIND AND LETTING GO of the heavy stuff is easier said than done. Instead of trying to do a huge fucking overhaul and emotional spring cleaning, try for something smaller. Choose a solo activity or some sort of ritual. It could be going for a bike ride, meditating by some super-fucking-overpriced candles, or doing an art project.

What will you do?

_____

_____

_____

_____

How often can you do it?

_____

_____

_____

_____

Make note of how you feel afterward.

_____

_____

_____

_____

Running with SCISSORS

BOREDOM AND ACCESS TO SHARP OBJECTS are not a fantastic combo. While not everyone is a danger to society by running through life with miniature swords, there are times when you can feel like you're making haphazard decisions, running amok, and generally being a pain in the ass to others.

USE THOSE SCISSORS FOR THE BETTER!

What are the things you can cut out that don't
add anything positive to your world?

Snip snip that shit!

BE NICE, ASSHOLE!

NO MATTER WHAT YOU DO, you can't turn that curmudgeon, that colossal douchebag, or that hate-breathing dragon in your life into a better or more pleasant person. But, you can let the beautiful buttercup inside you blossom. So, surround yourself with nice things. Like these flowers.

Color these fucking flowers.
AND BE NICE TO PEOPLE!

STOP *and* SMELL *the* INCENSE

IT'S EASY TO BE IN A CONSTANT WHIRLWIND and not notice the things around you. Whether you do this literally or figuratively, use the length of time it takes to burn an incense stick (a whopping 30 minutes) to chill the fuck out without any distractions.

Where do your thoughts go?

What good things surround you?

Describe what you're seeing, and what about it can make you feel at ease.

WELL, WELL, WELL...
Check it out! It's a wellness wheel!

Starting from the center of the wheel and working out, color in each wedge based on where you think you are with the subject. Do you feel super healthy and happy when you think about your body? Shade the fuck out of "Beautiful You." Do you wish you had more time with family? Scribble in a small portion of "Forced Fam Fun."

What gives?

When you look at your wellness wheel, what are you most excited about filling in more? How can you make it happen?

_____

_____

_____

_____

_____

Happy Vibes

Work-Life-Balance + Shit

Love + Sex

Friendship!

Catching Zs + Relaxation

Forced Fam Fun

Beautiful You

"THINK LIKE A QUEEN.

A QUEEN IS NOT AFRAID TO FAIL. FAILURE IS ANOTHER STEPPINGSTONE TO GREATNESS."

—OPRAH WINFREY

Imagine that you're the queen or king of fucking everything. What risks would you take that you wouldn't right now?

What good things do you keep putting off until later, when you have more time or more money? How could you build them into your happy little kingdom right now?

HAPPY HEARTS

There is a fuck-ton of outside pressure telling you to be in the perfect relationship, to post the cutest photos, and to hit your relationship landmarks. But the reality is that none of these things will be perfect, on time, or necessarily exactly how you imagine them to be. If you're in a relationship or if you're doing your own thing— what are the things about it that make your heart happy? Who fills you with love?

Write it between the hearts.

DOORMAT, SHMOORMAT!

SOME PEOPLE ARE DOORMATS, some people scuff their feet all over the fucking place, but everyone has done their share of both at one point or another. Below, make a list of those times when you've been a doormat, and the times when you've tracked your muddy-ass feet on others.

Now, be fucking hospitable!

Come up with your own welcome mats. Show positive vibes for the people you've welcomed into your life to show them you care, as well as friendly reminders to others not to tread their feet on you.

THE WATER'S WARM

KINDLY TRACK YOUR MUD ELSEWHERE

SURPRISE, SURPRISE!

SOME SURPRISES ARE FUN AND EXCITING, and some surprises cause fucking heart attacks. For now, let's stick with the happy confetti kind. What are some ways that you could switch up your routine, talk to someone new, or open yourself up to a little serendipity?

Scoot the fuck over and make room for the unexpected.

MAKE
TIME,
BE
PRESENT

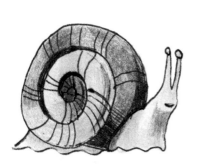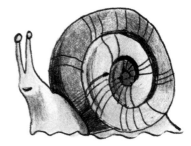

BUELLER... BUELLER...

YOU CAN'T EXPECT PEOPLE TO ADORE YOUR UNIQUE IDEAS and charming-as-fuck personality if you don't give them the time of day. Appreciate the people around you, dammit! Who are the people you want in your circles? How can you be present for them in your relationship? Use the circles to make these lists, and color them in, too!

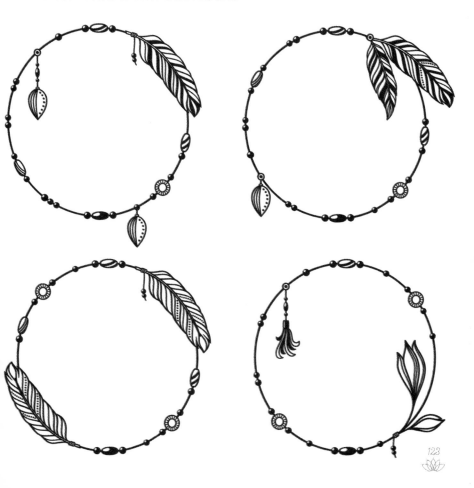

Namaste, MOTHERFUCKER!

While this long, winding, and profanity-driven journey may have brought some opportunities to stop giving a fuck about the bullshit plague upon your existence, it's also speckled with hope for finding the happiest of good things.

What are the most fucking divine things you can find in yourself along this path? What about other people? Bow to them by writing them in the diagram to the right.

Take it all in. Smile, if you please.
Cast your soul-shining light
on others and make your world
a little fucking beautiful.

YOU

OTHERS

ACKNOWLEDGMENTS

MY WARMEST THANK-YOUS go out to Aimee Chase, Katie Jennings Campbell, Holly Schmidt, Allan Penn, Bruce Lubin, Marisa Bartlett, and Jennifer Leight—who are endlessly and hyperbolically supportive, collaborative, and patient, and without whom I would not have a platform for positive profanity. Thank you to Andy Martin, Nichole Argyres, Courtney Littler, Amelie Littell, and the rest of the fantastic team at St. Martin's Press for making great books and for generally doing the impossible. Special hugs to Katie Sweeney for enduring lifelong sisterhood and for being so aggressively encouraging all the time.

ABOUT THE AUTHOR

Monica Sweeney is a writer and editor.
She lives in Boston, Massachusetts.